285
as is

Tape
on
cover

Imagine That!
It's Modern Dance

By STEPHANIE RIVA SORINE

Photographs by
DANIEL S. SORINE

Alfred A. Knopf
New York

This is a Borzoi Book
Published by Alfred A. Knopf, Inc.

Published in the United States by Alfred A. Knopf, Inc.,
New York, and simultaneously in Canada by Random House of
Canada Limited, Toronto.
Distributed by Random House, Inc., New York.
Library of Congress Cataloging in Publication Data
Sorine, Stephanie Riva.
Imagine that! It's modern dance.
Summary: Three young dancers present some modern dance
vocabulary—objects, actions, directions, sizes,
shapes, feelings, and ideas.
1. Modern dance—Juvenile literature. [1. Modern dance]
I. Sorine, Daniel S., joint author.   II. Title.
GV1783.S67   1981   793.3′2   80-19232
ISBN 0-394-84474-2 (Tr.)   ISBN 0-394-94474-7 (lib. bdg.)
Designed by Mina Greenstein
Manufactured in the United States of America
1 3 5 7 9 0 8 6 4 2

Thank you very much Pat Ross!
And thank you Andrea Brown, Linn Fischer
and Mina Greenstein....Being published at
Alfred A. Knopf is a great pleasure.

Grateful acknowledgment to the children
who "dance" in this book: Laura Dishman,
Jessica Holmes and Vanessa Rhee.

Dedicated to the dancer in all of us.

Stephanie and Daniel Sorine

Hello!
How do you do?

*I*t's no surprise that modern dance is growing more popular all the time. Modern dance is a delight to be a part of, or to watch. It encourages freedom: The dancer's freedom to express something and the viewer's freedom to interpret.

"Hello! How are you?"

"I feel great!" you say, using words to express how you feel. Modern dancers use gestures and body movement instead of words to answer this same question. Their dancing "talks" about many things: action, direction, sizes and shapes, objects, feelings, ideas. Through dancing, their poses suggest how something acts, looks, and feels.

Laura Dishman, Jessica Holmes, and Vanessa Rhee, the dancers in this book, portray just some of the many movements of modern dance. They show you an expression. You may feel what they feel, or something different. Modern dance is never just one thing.

A dancer whose body is "straight and sharp" may be an arrow to one person and a rocket to the next. A quiet pose may suggest gentleness, melting, or sleep itself. Modern dance is whatever *you* see—whatever *you* want it to be. So much depends on how you react to the dancers' special language.

Explore this freedom in *Imagine That! It's Modern Dance.* Discover modern dance, and let your imagination run in many directions.

Stephanie Riva Sorine

MODERN DANCE:
It's whatever you see.

It could be the letter T...

stacked chairs,

a bridg

two trees and a hammock,

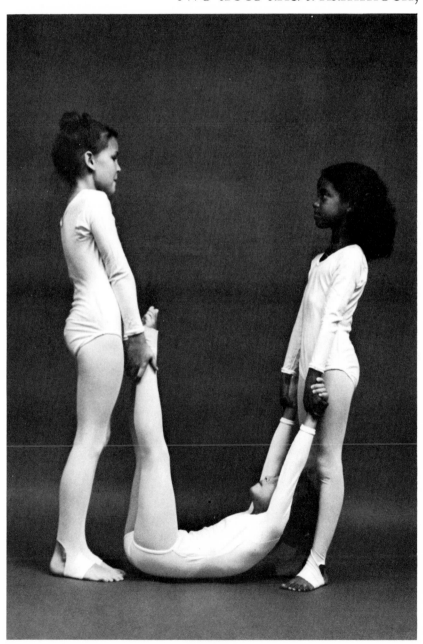

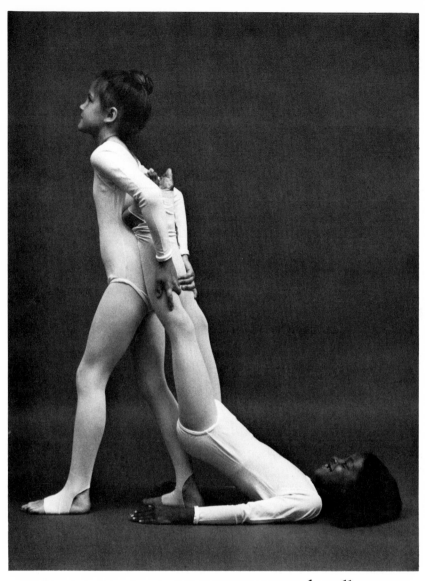

a wheelbarrow,

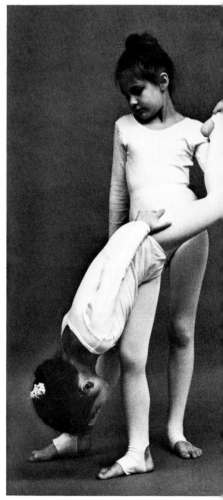

a squeaky water pump

a tunnel,

a towering lamppost,

a TV antenna,

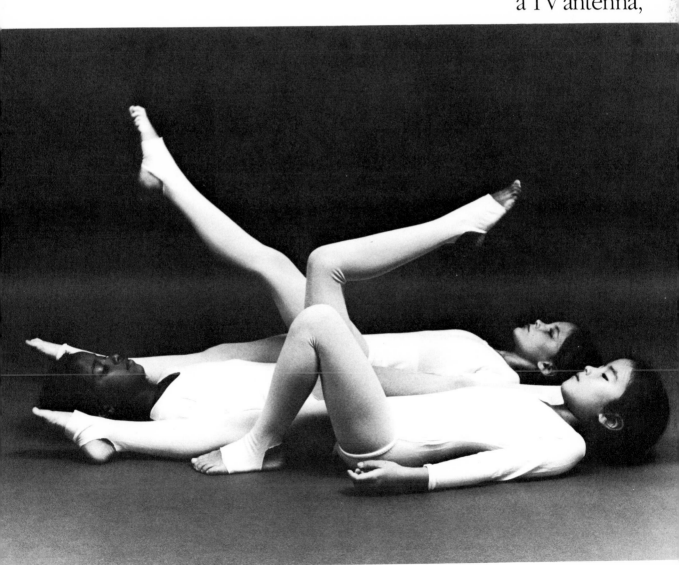

a bow and...

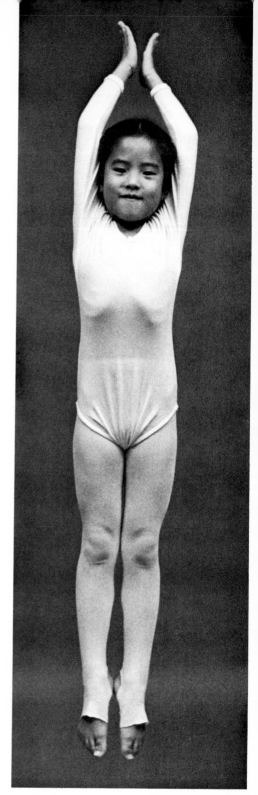

arrow,
so straight
and sharp.

Choochoo-Choochoo-Choochoo.

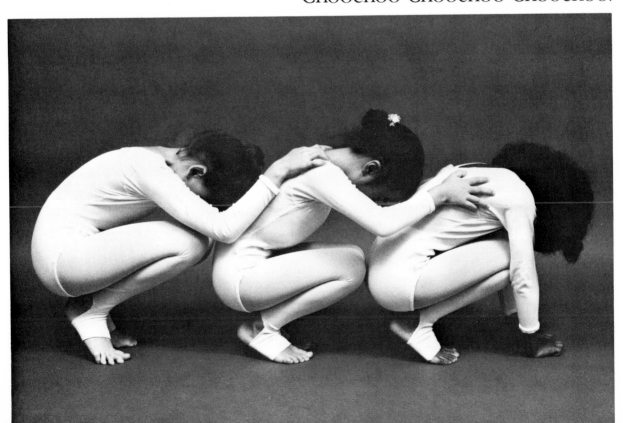

Stop! That's not all.

MODERN DANCE:

It's action.

Reaching...

crouching,

growing,

twisting,

diving,

bending,

perching,

whirling and twirling.

It's tilting, too.

MODERN DANCE:

It's direction.

Going forward,

backward,

side to side,

down,

up,

and across.

MODERN DANCE:
It's all shapes and sizes.

metimes it's circular,

angular,

triangular,

rectangular,

and curved.

It can be wide

or closed so tight.

Then suddenly it's open.

MODERN DANCE:

It's all kinds of feelings.

Sleepy.

Playful.

Lonely.

Carefree.

Or simply serious.

Rough and tough!
It's about these feelings
and many more.

MODERN DANCE:

You might see...

a sailboat gliding,

a jet taking off,

branches swaying in the wind,

a plant pushing through the soil,

honey flowing from a jar.

Kites soar.

Books end.

Imagine that!

Stephanie Riva Sorine grew up in Woodbury, Long Island. She trained at the School of American Ballet and London's Royal Ballet School, danced as a soloist with the Austrian Ballet, and apprenticed with the Harkness Ballet. She teaches classes in ballet and dance movement to children and adults in New York City.

Daniel S. Sorine was born in Paris, France and raised in Monaco. He studied at Le Rosey and Institut Florimont in Switzerland and Lycée Français de New York. His photographs have appeared in *Life, Time, Newsweek, People, TV Guide, The New York Times, Dancemagazine, New West,* and in other publications in America and abroad.

The Sorines, who now live in New York City, have been married since 1977, and are the authors of *At Every Turn! It's Ballet,* as well as the highly acclaimed adult book, *Dancershoes,* and Ballantine's ballet calendars.